# Dedication

This work is dedicated to every young mind determined to break free from the chains of miseducation. To the students who question, the teachers who empower, and the ancestors whose sacrifices paved the road we walk today.

May this guide serve as a light, a weapon, and a foundation.
Never forget — you were born to lead, not follow.
The world is your classroom. The truth is your legacy.

- Cedric A. Washington
Author. Educator. Revolutionary.

The MISEDUCATION of the Negro in the 21st Century – College/University Student Workbook

Who Lives Like This?! Publishing LLC
www.nerdyouthservices.org

ISBN: 978-1-970680-05-8 (Hardback)

Cover design and interior layout by
Who Lives Like This?! Publishing LLC Design Team

Printed in the United States of America

First Edition — 2025

## About the Author

Cedric A. Washington is a master educator, speaker, author, former college basketball player, and the Executive Director of NERD Youth Services, Inc. A native of Gary, Indiana. Over two decades of experience in education, mentoring, and community leadership have fueled his commitment to building culturally responsive, empowering programs for African American youth. The MISEDUCATION of the Negro in the 21st Century: College/University Student Workbook is a rigorous, text-derived academic companion designed for use in higher education classrooms, seminars, and independent study. Authored by Washington, this workbook challenges students to confront modern systems of miseducation operating within schools, politics, religion, culture, and identity formation.

Unlike traditional workbooks, this is a thinking document, not a worksheet packet. Every prompt, writing task, and reflection is derived directly from the core text and requires students to engage critically with the author's language, metaphors, and arguments. Students are expected to analyze power, privilege, compliance, institutional control, and intellectual conditioning as they appear in contemporary education and society.

Structured for college-level rigor, the workbook emphasizes long-form analytical writing, seminar preparation, textual evidence, and synthesis across chapters. It is aligned with the Professor's Edition and integrates the Knowledge of S.E.L.F. (Social Empowerment Learning Framework), guiding students through self-awareness, social consciousness, and intellectual accountability.

This workbook is ideal for courses in African American Studies, Education, Sociology, Social Justice, Cultural Studies, and Political Science. Discomfort is expected. Silence is permitted. Growth is required.

# THE MISEDUCATION OF THE NEGRO

## IN THE 21ST CENTURY

### COLLEGE / UNIVERSITY STUDENT WORKBOOK

**Text-Derived Workbook**
Aligned with the Professor's Edition
Teach Like Ced Series
Knowledge of S.E.L.F. (Social Empowerment Learning Framework)

---

## STUDENT INSTRUCTIONS

This workbook is not a worksheet packet.
It is a **thinking document**.

Every response must:

- come from the assigned chapter
- reference the author's language
- reflect critical engagement

Discomfort is expected.
Silence is permitted.
Growth is required.

---

# PREFACE — STUDENT WORKBOOK

**Close Reading Focus**

(Use the Preface text only)

**Key Concepts (from the text)**

- miseducation
- cultural competency
- institutional control
- data-driven discipline
- compliance vs. consciousness

- freedom
- intellectual slavery

---

## Written Response 1 (2–3 pages)

Using the Preface, explain how **state standards and mainstream curriculum** restrict culturally competent teaching.
Use the author's metaphors (water into wine, soul food, Hennessey) to support your response.

**Written Response 2 (2 pages)**

Analyze the author's statement:

"Schools pride themselves on a model versus listening to the expert."

How does this reflect **miseducation**?

_____

_____

_____

_____

_____

_____

_____

_____

_____

_____

_____

_____

_____

**Seminar Preparation Page**

List **three moments** in the Preface where the author identifies:

- control
- compliance
- punishment

Explain why each moment matters.

_____

_____

_____

_____

_____

_____

_____

_____

_____

_____

# CHAPTER 1 — PRIVILEGE

## Text-Derived Vocabulary

(use author context)

- privilege
- charter schools
- miseducation
- psychological enslavement
- access
- constitutional promise

## Analytical Writing (3 pages)

Explain why the author frames **privilege** as more than money.
How does privilege function historically and psychologically in education?

# Critical Reflection (2 pages)

What responsibility does the author place on **white liberal teachers**?
Support your response using only the chapter.

# CHAPTER 2 — FIGUREHEAD

## Key Terms (from text)

- figurehead
- authority
- badge of honor
- job security
- exploitation
- school-to-prison pipeline

## Seminar Writing (3 pages)

Explain how Black principals are positioned as **figureheads**.
How does miseducation operate at the leadership level?

**Application Page (2 pages)**

Connect **figurehead leadership** to your own educational experiences.

_____
_____
_____
_____
_____
_____
_____
_____
_____
_____
_____
_____
_____
_____
_____
_____
_____
_____
_____
_____
_____
_____

# CHAPTER 3 — KNOWLEDGE VS. EDUCATION

## Core Language

- knowledge
- education
- identity
- cognitive dissonance
- self-awareness
- culture

# Extended Essay (4 pages)

Using the chapter, explain why **education without knowledge is slavery**.
Include:

- CASEL critique
- identity omission
- cultural disconnect

# CHAPTER 4 — CULTURE = INTELLIGENCE = BEHAVIOR

## Concept Mapping (2 pages)

Using the author's framework, map how:

- culture
- produces intelligence
- which produces behavior

_____
_____
_____
_____
_____
_____
_____
_____
_____
_____

## Analytical Writing (3 pages)

Explain how historical trauma continues to shape modern behavior.
Use examples directly from the chapter.

_____
_____
_____
_____
_____
_____
_____
_____
_____
_____

# CHAPTER 5 — PARENTS AND THE ENVIRONMENT

## Key Language

- rearing
- environment
- accountability
- misinformed adults
- community

## Reflection + Analysis (4 pages)

How do parents and environment perpetuate miseducation?
Explain how **accountability has shifted** over generations.

# CHAPTER 6 — HIP-HOP

## Core Language

- culture
- narrative
- exploitation
- master/slave
- House Negro / Field Negro

## Cultural Analysis (4 pages)

Using the chapter only, analyze how Hip-Hop both **educates and miseducates**.

# CHAPTER 7 — POLITICS

## Key Concepts

- Black agenda
- voting
- power
- dependency
- unity

## Analytical Essay (4 pages)

Why does political participation not equal liberation?
Use historical examples cited by the author.

# CHAPTER 8 — THE BLACK CHURCH

## Text Language

- religion
- control
- obedience
- separation of church and state
- miseducation

---

## Theological Analysis (4 pages)

Explain how religion has been used to **control and pacify** rather than liberate.
Remain text-faithful.

# CHAPTER 9 — REVELATION

## Core Language

- revelation
- four hundred years
- awakening
- truth
- identity

---

## Capstone Writing (6 pages)

Using Chapter 9 only, explain how **revelation disrupts miseducation**.

This is your final synthesis.

# FINAL SELF REFLECTION (Knowledge of S.E.L.F.)

## Extended Reflection (4 pages)

Which area of SELF mastery was most challenged by this text?

- SELF Conscience
- SELF Governing
- Social Conscience
- Aspirations
- Good People Skills

Explain using **author language only**.

_____
_____
_____
_____
_____
_____
_____
_____
_____
_____
_____
_____
_____
_____
_____
_____
_____
_____
_____
_____
_____
_____
_____
_____
_____
_____
_____
_____

www.ingramcontent.com/pod-product-compliance
Lightning Source LLC
Chambersburg PA
CBHW082112040426
42335CB00040B/2821